OWEN McCAFFERTY

Born in 1961, Owen lives with his wife and three children in Belfast. His work includes *Shoot the Crow* (Druid, Galway, 1997; Royal Exchange, Manchester, 2003; Trafalgar Studios, London, 2005); *Mojo Mickybo* (Kabosh, Belfast, 1998); *Closing Time* (National Theatre, London, 2002); *Scenes from the Big Picture* (National Theatre, London, 2003); *Days of Wine and Roses* (Donmar Warehouse, London, 2005) and *Antigone* (Ulster Bank Festival at Queen's, 2008). All of these plays are published by Nick Hern Books, including *Cold Comfort* which appears in an anthology of one-man plays, *Singular (Male) Voices*. He has won the Meyer-Whitworth, the John Whiting and the Evening Standard Awards for New Playwriting.

JP Miller's

DAYS OF WINE
AND ROSES

in a new version by

Owen McCafferty

NICK HERN BOOKS
London
www.nickhernbooks.co.uk

A Nick Hern Book

This version of JP Miller's *Days of Wine and Roses* first published in
Great Britain in 2005 as a paperback original by Nick Hern Books Limited,
14 Larden Road, London W3 7ST

Reprinted 2011

Typeset by Country Setting, Kingsdown, Kent, CT14 8ES
Printed in the UK by CLE Print Ltd, St Ives, Cambs, PE27 3LE

A CIP catalogue record for this book is available from the British Library

ISBN   978 1 85459 858 5

World Premiere

J P Miller's *Days of Wine and Roses*
in a new version by Owen McCafferty
was first commissioned and developed by
SCAMP Film and Theatre Ltd and
RJK Productions, Inc.

First performance at the Donmar Warehouse, London,
on 17 February 2005, with the following cast:

Anne-Marie Duff and Peter McDonald

Directed by Peter Gill
Designed by Alison Chitty
Lighting by Hartley T.A. Kemp
Music by Terry Davies
Sound by Matt McKenzie

for those whose light shines brightly

if only for a brief moment

Characters

DONAL, *mid-twenties*

MONA, *mid-twenties*

The play takes place between 1962 and 1970.

Throughout the play the actors should remain onstage.

Scene One

1962. Belfast Airport departure lounge.

DONAL. planes

MONA. sorry

DONAL. planes – we're not meant to be up there – birds aren't that size – that should tell us something shouldn't it

MONA. if they can orbit the moon i'm sure flying to london won't be a problem

DONAL. you're going london

MONA. yes

DONAL. me too – my name's donal by the way – donal mackin

MONA. mona mcreynolds

DONAL. mona – nice name – you don't mind me talking to you mona do you – people can be funny about strangers talking to them

MONA. not at all – talk away

DONAL. have they said how long we're going to be delayed

MONA. no – just waiting for the wind to die down

DONAL. you'd think a good strong wind would be of some type of benefit to the whole notion of flying – do you believe that stuff about the moon

MONA. it was in the paper

DONAL. you shouldn't believe everything you read in the paper

MONA. i don't

DONAL. i think it's a con

MONA. why

DONAL. don't know – haven't worked that out yet – i just know that whenever i look up at the moon the first thing that strikes me is that it's not a stones throw away

MONA. i'd like it to be true – the thought of it is exciting – being able to fly up into space – maybe one day we'll all be able to do that

DONAL. i'll give you whatever odds you like that's never going to happen

MONA. it will – there's no point in them going up there otherwise

DONAL. strong winds hardly stop that flight – sorry no rocket flight today lads the wind would blow you away out there

MONA. we could all take our holidays on a space ship

DONAL. a space ship – jesus – a space ship – something about that doesn't sound right either – you been over in london before

MONA. no – you

DONAL. no – first time in the big city – be a bit different from belfast i'd say

MONA. i hope so

DONAL. you just going over for a holiday to visit relatives or something

MONA. no – i don't have any relatives there – i'm going over to live

DONAL. so am i

MONA. have you people there

DONAL. no – i'm going to be all on my swanny – it's to do with work

MONA. your company transferring you over there

DONAL. sort of but not really – i work in a bookies here in belfast – mchughs – just round the corner from the cattle market – you know it

MONA. i think i've passed it once or twice

DONAL. i clerk for a bookie at race meetings as well – all over ireland – i do the dogs too – it's a small outfit – the man that owns it knows that i really should be manager now – but he wants to keep running it himself – he says it gives him something to do – and if he wasn't doin it he'd be stuck at home with the wife

MONA. maybe she doesn't want to be stuck at home with him

DONAL. he's joking when he says that

MONA. oh

DONAL. anyway – my boss has contacts with a bigger outfit in london – they were looking for a manager and he put a good word in for me – so that's what i'm going over to do – manage a bookies

MONA. it was good of him to help you like that

DONAL. it was – although in saying that he owed me

MONA. it's normally the other way round isn't it

DONAL. what

MONA. people owe bookies

DONAL. there's not many of them that's skint that's true – he owed me because i'm very good at what i do – born to it you might say – when i started there the place was a kip and i turned it round for him – he thought it was just about figures but it's not – my da taught me to always make your work social – so that's what i do – i get on well with the punters – i'm good with the figures part as well – you need both

MONA. is your father a bookie

DONAL. no he drives a tram

MONA. i'd love to do that

DONAL. drive a tram

MONA. yes – why not

DONAL. no reason – not something you think of women doing though

MONA. doesn't mean you shouldn't do it

DONAL. what do you do

MONA. work in the civil service

DONAL. good job – steady

MONA. yes – steady

DONAL. that's what you're going over to london to do is it

MONA. i suppose so – there's a job waiting on me – i don't know though – we'll see what happens

DONAL. have you something else in mind

MONA. not really – work isn't really the reason i'm going over to london

DONAL. oh i see

MONA. you see what

DONAL. sorry i shouldn't have said anything – it's none of my business

MONA. you think i'm pregnant don't you

DONAL. sorry – i didn't mean – it's just you hear that a lot of girls go over to london because

MONA. i'm not

DONAL. it's ok – really it's ok

MONA. really i'm not – all i meant was that the reason i'm going to london isn't to do with work – it's personal

DONAL. i understand

MONA. no you don't – you think i mean bad personal – i mean personal in that it has to do with me

DONAL. right – you don't have to tell me anything – we're just sitting here talking to pass the time – that's all

MONA. i know that – i just had this feeling one day that going to london was something i had to do

DONAL. the bright lights

MONA. something like that

DONAL. all on that journey to make our fortunes

MONA. no not that – i just had this feeling one morning
walking to work that i didn't want to be in belfast any more
– it felt like it was too small and that i knew everything
about it – and all that i knew i didn't really like

DONAL. sometimes there's not too much to like about it
you're right about that

MONA. i felt like i didn't want to die there – or maybe it was
if i stayed there i would die – my parents think i'm mad –
they probably thought that anyway

DONAL (*takes a hip flask from his coat*). do you mind if i
have a drink – a quick nip to warm the cockles of your heart

MONA. not at all go ahead

DONAL. do you want one

MONA. no thanks i don't drink – it's a family thing – was
never any drink in our house – my father's a very
disciplined man – does the same things at the same time
every day – his father liked a drink and i think that put him
off – there's six of us – he wouldn't tell us not to drink but i
don't think he'd be happy if we did – so none of us touch it
– what you've never had you don't miss

DONAL. the other way of looking at that is – what you've
never had you don't know about – or – a little bit of
something does you good

MONA. would you like me to have a drink

DONAL. you could look back upon this as a good memory –
the day that i was starting out my new life in london i met
this very nice young man called donal – i had my first drink
with him and it was a laugh – when you're an old woman
sitting talking to all your cats that will be a good memory

MONA. i don't like cats

DONAL. i don't like drinking on my own

MONA. since you put it that way why not – (*Drinks.*) – that's
awful

DONAL *(drinks)*. you get used to it – well – you make
yourself get used to it – i used to be a pioneer – but then
given the line of work i'm in it's just too difficult not to
have a drink – after race meetings you spend a lot of time
in pubs and that – drinking's the price you have to pay for
getting on in this game

MONA. do your parents think you're mad going to london

DONAL. no – they see it as an opportunity to make a better
life for myself – sad to see me go but glad that i was going

MONA. it was because this all happened on the spare of the
moment that my father thinks i'm mad – it didn't fit in with
the discipline thing you see – he can't get his head round
things like that

DONAL. i understand him – i don't do things on the spare of
the moment – *(She kisses him.)*

MONA. it's ok go on

DONAL. i need to know what's happening – i need to work
things out – i've been in contact – are you going to do that
again

MONA. might – keep talking

DONAL. i've been in contact with the people i'll be working
for about six times already – making sure it's all settled and
done and ok – i've looked at street maps of london – make
sure i know where i'm going

MONA. you don't always need to know where you're going – i
have somewhere to stay for a few days but i don't know
exactly where it is – in brixton somewhere – when i was
thinking about it i could see myself getting off the train and
just walking about for a while until i found the place

DONAL. i'll know where it is – it'll be alright i'll get you
there

MONA. no i don't want to know where it is – i like the idea i
don't know where it is

DONAL. it all has to do with information

MONA. what has to do with information

DONAL. in my work i deal with a lot of facts and figures – the more information you get the more you need – information tells you about things – the more you know about things the more you are in control – the more you are in control the more you need to be in control

MONA. i don't care – just let me walk around the streets of london for a while not knowing where i'm going

He hands her the hip flask. She drinks.

DONAL. getting any easier

MONA. no

DONAL. it will

MONA. you say

DONAL. i say – there's this horse

MONA. is this a joke – i don't really get jokes

DONAL. no – you're going to end up walking about london for weeks not a penny on you – but i have a plan to save you – i have a foolproof way of getting money – i'm going to give you the name of a horse

MONA. foolproof way – a horse – very good

DONAL. oh yes – i'll give you the name of this horse – the bookies where i'm working is in the elephant and castle – it's called dobbs – you go there and put money on this horse

MONA. how can i if i'm skint

DONAL. good point

MONA. the bookies isn't the place for a nice young girl like myself

DONAL. right – i'll tell you about the horse anyway – mullingar – lough ennel plate – 3rd – leopardstown – greystones flat race – 4th – navan – bective novice hurdle – won – naas – rathconnel handicap hurdle – won – baldoyle – balbriggan handicap hurdle – won – fairyhouse – new handicap hurdle – won – dundalk – wee county handicap

hurdle – won – gowan park – president's handicap hurdle –
won – right – that's this horse's form so far – and on top of
that he comes from a good stable – this horse is a champion
– be over here next week for the honeybourne chase at
cheltenham – put your tank on it – arkle – that's what you
call the horse – remember i was the first one to tell you that
– punters follow this horse they'll make a fortune – arkle

MONA. arkle

DONAL. it's the name of a mountain in scotland or something
– i really don't like the idea of you walking about london on
your own

MONA. that's sweet – but don't say it again – this is my new
start – it's up to me what i do – free as a bird – i'm having
my first drink aren't i

DONAL. alright – i'm going over here and see if there's any
word about the plane

MONA. yes you do that

DONAL *exits.* MONA *takes a drink from the hip flask.*
DONAL *returns.*

DONAL. not long maybe about another half hour

MONA. what about this for an idea

DONAL. by the way i asked if we could be seated together –
you don't mind

MONA. no i don't mind

DONAL. your idea

MONA. yes – what about whenever we get to london you
forget that you know everywhere and we could walk round
brixton together – do you think that's a good idea

DONAL. i don't know everywhere

MONA. donal – just say whether you think it's a good idea or
not

DONAL. i think it's a good idea mona

MONA. so do i

Scene Two

1963. MONA *standing on Westminster Bridge looking out over the river. It is early evening.* DONAL *arrives.*

DONAL. sorry you haven't been waiting here long have you – one of the punters touched for a big bet – wanted to bring all the staff out for a drink

MONA. it's alright – i don't mind – i like westminster bridge – this is where i come when we're not out together

DONAL. here

MONA. yes

DONAL. you stand here on your own

MONA. yes

DONAL. i don't like that – something could happen to you

MONA. don't be silly

DONAL. you never know what could happen

MONA. yes i do

DONAL. what could happen

MONA. the same as what always happens – nothing – something did happen one night

DONAL. you see – what happened – what night

MONA. it was something but it was nothing – nobody ever speaks to me – but this night a man did – he asked me was everything alright – he said sometimes people need to talk – he said it's not a good thing not to talk – i must have looked lonely i think

DONAL. and were you – you shouldn't be – i'm here

MONA. i wasn't – not really

DONAL. not really

MONA. i don't like sitting in my room alone – it frightens me more than it does out walking the streets

DONAL. i don't like the idea of you being frightened

MONA. it's not in the way you think – i don't think i'm in danger – it's just – i don't know – you must feel alone sometimes – maybe it's not alone – maybe it's just being on my own

DONAL. i never get a chance to be on my own – working morning noon and night since i got here

MONA. it doesn't matter – you're here now that's what's important

DONAL. is that what's important

MONA. yes

DONAL. good – the longer you're here the more your group of friends expands

MONA. we're meeting people later on aren't we

DONAL. you know me so well – i told george we'd meet him for a drink – he is the boss – i don't like knocking him back

MONA. you can't knock him back – it's business

DONAL. correct – he wants to introduce us to another couple anyway

MONA. we must look lonely to everyone who sets eyes on us do we

DONAL. he just wants to make it easier to settle in that's all – that's a good thing isn't it

MONA. i didn't say it wasn't – does he think of you as us

DONAL. i don't know – i think of us as us – do you not

MONA. think of you as us or us as us or me as us

DONAL. you thinking of you as us is the same as me thinking of me as us

MONA. i knew i was right

DONAL. what

MONA. i was sitting in work today – bored to the point of distraction – to relieve the boredom i started to think of you

DONAL. i'm glad i am of some use

MONA. i was trying to work out what it is i find attractive about you

DONAL. i'm sure there are many things

MONA. i have to be honest about this donal there aren't – it came down to two things

DONAL. could one of them be the fact that i'm not easily offended

MONA. three things then

DONAL. three things that are attractive or a choice of three and you could only find one

MONA. that

DONAL. right – do i need to sit down for this

MONA. it's your brains

DONAL. not the good looks

MONA. they weren't even on the shortlist of three

DONAL. i'm heartbroken – what's my poor old mummy going to say – ugly but smart – i'm sure that's not what she tells everyone in the street – (*He puts his arms around her.*) – right – have we to be honest here – because you know how i hate that

MONA. try it just for me

DONAL. alright here we go – you know what i find attractive about you

MONA. yes

DONAL. yes – no – no

MONA. alright besides the fact that i'm really pretty – no

DONAL. everything – everything all the time

MONA (*kisses him*). what do you call the couple we're going to meet

DONAL. dave and doris

MONA. donal – dave – doris – i should change my name to something beginning with d

DONAL. don't rush in – wait until we see how we get on with them first – have you eaten

MONA. i thought we were going out for something to eat

DONAL. we are

MONA. then why would i have eaten

DONAL. i don't know i just asked

MONA. why

DONAL. is this a quiz – if i answer all your questions correctly will i win money or a cooker or something

MONA. what would you do with a cooker

DONAL. is this one of the questions – i'd sell it – is that the right answer

MONA. yes

DONAL. we'll go and get something to eat

MONA. we've time yet – i like standing here – i like standing here with you – what are dave and doris like – have you met them before

DONAL. no – i've seen a photograph of them

MONA. how did they look

DONAL. happy – they were at a dinner dance george had invited them to – so they would look happy – we'll see them later – it's not a big deal mona

MONA. you just like to know these things – and it might be a big deal – these people could be our lifelong friends

DONAL. assuming we're lifelong friends that is

MONA. we could do something about that

DONAL. what way

MONA. marry me

DONAL. what

MONA. don't what

DONAL. it's sudden – that deserves a what

MONA. not awkward

DONAL. awkward

MONA. me asking you – i don't want this to be a big thing

DONAL. it is a big thing

MONA. no not like that – i mean a big thing as in out of
nowhere – it isn't out of nowhere – i hope it isn't

DONAL. no it isn't

MONA. i was thinking – it's like – look – i know that you love
me – i just felt – i felt that because of the way you are
sometimes that it might take you longer than it should – to
say the things you want to say – or ask the questions you
want to ask – so today i was thinking that i should maybe
give you a hand with that – don't be angry with me for
doing that – i would die if you were

DONAL. why in god's name would i be angry

MONA. i don't know – you might – i feel like i'm going to cry
now – i shouldn't have said this

DONAL. please don't cry

MONA. i won't – i meant i don't know whether you would get
angry or not because i don't know everything about you –
and i said what i said because i want to know everything
about you – oh god – can we start again

DONAL. right

MONA. right

Silence.

DONAL. mona will you marry me

MONA. no

DONAL. what

MONA. well anybody that has to be forced into doing
something – it isn't really the best start is it

DONAL. mona

MONA. yes

DONAL. yes yes

MONA. yes – yes yes – we need to celebrate – get your flask out

DONAL. it's empty i drank it earlier on

MONA. why

DONAL. george and the lads bet me i couldn't drink it down in one go – it doesn't matter we'll go somewhere and get a drink

MONA. no i don't want to go somewhere – i want it to happen here – it's a moment – it needs to happen here

DONAL. alright – what other way than having a drink is there to celebrate

MONA. why don't you keep a back-up flask

DONAL. you want me to walk about with two flasks on me – i'm not sure but that might give off the wrong signals to people – anyway if you knew you were going to do this why didn't you bring a drink

MONA. because drink's your department

DONAL. we have departments now – the words about marriage have barely left our mouths and already we have departments – i suppose i'll have to go out and get the coal all the time will i

MONA. yes the coal would be one of your departments – i can't believe there's no way of celebrating without a drink – what do people who never drink do

DONAL. people who never drink have nothing to celebrate about

MONA. do this

MONA *throws her arms in the air and jumps up and down. She stops waiting for* DONAL *to do it. He does. She continues. They laugh.*

DONAL. is that our thing now

MONA. our thing

DONAL. people have their song and that – is that our thing

MONA. might be

They jump up and down again, then kiss.

DONAL. how important is food do you think

MONA. you're such a cheapskate

DONAL. nothing to do with money – i don't feel in the mood for eating now – i think we should go and have a drink and a good laugh – meet up with the rest of them later on – but only if you're alright with that

MONA. say mrs mackin

DONAL. mrs mackin

MONA. i'm alright with anything that you're alright with mr mackin – and that's the way it is from now on

Scene Three

1964. DONAL and MONA's flat. MONA is offstage putting the baby to bed. DONAL enters. He carries a bag with bottles of drink in it. The newspaper is sticking out of his coat pocket. He has obviously already had a few drinks. He is singing 'Slievenamon'.

DONAL. 'and the hall it is gay and the waves they are grand – but my heart is not there at all – it flies far away by night and by day' – where are the people – where are the lovely wife and the beautiful child on this day of all days

MONA enters. She is tired.

MONA. keep the noise down i've just got him over

DONAL. my love – the love of my life

MONA. i take it the horse won

DONAL. the horse – what is that the horse – arkle is a god – i worship the ground he gallops over – i have to go in and say goodnight to my son – the boy

MONA. donal don't you'll wake him – it took me ages to get him over

DONAL. it must be done – on this day never to be forgotten – (*He takes the newspaper from his coat pocket and throws it in the air.*) march the seventh nineteen hundred and sixty-four – i must see the boy – so in years to come i can tell him that on the day arkle became a god – i stood over his cot while he was sleeping and whispered to him – sleep the sleep of the gods young man for today we are all kings – it must be said

MONA. don't wake him donal i mean it

DONAL *exits.* MONA *examines the bag and puts all the bottles of drink on the table. The baby cries.* DONAL *enters.*

jesus christ

DONAL. sorry – that child is beautiful like you

MONA. being beautiful doesn't stop him crying – (*Exits.*)

DONAL. the boy and the lady – and the man – i am the man (*He removes his coat and dances over to the table. He takes banknotes all rolled up into small balls from various pockets and puts them on the table. He pours himself a drink.*) the money trick – they're under starter's orders and they're off – lift them pinkie – i love this place – how can you not love this place – george doesn't know what he's doing – he has to be told – when you don't know what the score is you have to be wired off – that's my job

MONA *enters.*

george doesn't know what he's doing you know that

MONA. what's all the drink for

DONAL. to drink – you hear me what i said about george

MONA. yes – you haven't invited people round here have you

DONAL. yes – but listen stop talking a minute – he owns the place right – but when he's out on the course laying a book he's useless – he won't listen to me – he can't be told – i'm telling him what horses to lay off in order to balance the book – he says it's all about taking the risk – it's not – punters are meant to take the risk not the bookie – i'm going to have to speak to him

MONA. i don't want anybody round here tonight donal i'm exhausted

DONAL. it's only george and a few others – dave and doris – these are the people we want to know – these are the people we have to get on with – share this day with the people we need to know – this is the day – you have to understand the importance of this day

MONA. a horse won a race that's all

DONAL. no no no no – look sit down and have a drink – i'll explain all this before they arrive

MONA. why are you asking me to have a drink

DONAL. oh right – is that thing still going on

MONA. am i still breast-feeding you mean – yes – and he's going to be up for a feed in about four hours – which is why i don't want anyone here – i want to go to bed

DONAL. there's baby milk there – what's wrong with that

MONA. there's nothing wrong with it – it's just not what i wanted

DONAL. four months – come on – it's not that – it's not that – i don't want this to be a battle – this is a great day – i want this to be a great day – look – why are we here

MONA. why are we where

DONAL. here – london – here – why are we here – isn't this what it's all about – this now – we have what we wanted – how long have we been here – what – ah i don't know

MONA. seventeen months

DONAL. seventeen months – married – married to someone i love – we have a beautiful son – it hurts me to look at him

sometimes i love that child so much – and on top of that –
good times – the people i work with that come round here
are good people – good honest people – londoners – i love
them – we sing we dance we have a drink – good times – i
know over this last few months the baby takes up all of your
time – have a break from that – do what we came over here
to do

MONA. have a drink

DONAL. yes – but it isn't just that – it's more than that – live
the life that's here now in front of us – grasp it

MONA. your head's full of nonsense

DONAL. it's why you love me

MONA. pour me a drink (*He does.*)

DONAL. i said to you about george didn't i

MONA. yes donal you did

DONAL. i have to say to him – it's my duty to let him know
how the business should be run

MONA. you've a good job donal – don't blow it with this man

DONAL. i don't do things like that – mister don't blow it
that's me – he'll understand – he's a good man – right today
– you should have been there – i wanted you there beside
me – to feel what i was feeling – whenever kieran's older
we'll all go – right – the cheltenham gold cup – four
runners

MONA. pour me another drink before you start this (*He pours
both of them a drink. Takes the money from the table and
puts it on her lap.*)

DONAL. that's for you and the boy – readies – (*She kisses
him.*) – four runners – arkle – mill house – pas seul – and
king's nephew – only four runners because arkle and mill
house are a different class – the other two horses are top
notch – but what prices are they – twenty to one and fifty to
one – not a prayer between them – it would've froze you
solid today – the place is packed to the rafters – the irish are
hanging out of the woodwork – have to tell you this – this is

part of the importance of this – england's a great place –
london love it – londoners salt of the earth – the irish are for
arkle – the english are for mill house – this is a battle to the
death – before they go down to the off the horses are
parading round the paddock – you couldn't get moving for
punters trying to see arkle – you'd swear this horse knows it
too – once he hears the cheering it's as if he makes himself
bigger – then he holds his head up high – it's as if to say
here i am let the battle commence – this horse loves people
that's the only way i can describe it – this is another thing
too that made you realise that something special was going
to happen here – freezing – ten minutes before the off it
starts snowing – (MONA *pours herself another drink.*) –
then just as the horses are making their way down to the
start – it's like a gust of wind came and blew the snow away
– and there was the sun – a clear blue sky and a sun that lit
the whole of cheltenham – they're at the start – twenty
thousand punters – and four horses – they're under starter's
orders and they're off – twenty-one fences – three miles two
furlongs and a hundred and thirty yards – (*He becomes
animated, living the race.*) – all set off at a right clip – mill
house jumps the first in the lead – it's beautiful to see great
horses move – it's poetry – all jumping like they were born
for it – we're going downhill now – mill house is ahead by
about four lengths – you can see pat taffe is trying to hold
arkle back – he's not having an easy ride – doesn't want
arkle to go yet – too early – just hang in there – we're lying
forth but that's alright – mill house and pas seul are having
a bit of a tussle – good to watch but it's only the opening
act – mill house is jumping beautifully – arkle still in forth
but starting to make up ground now – pat taffe's just letting
him go a bit – just easing him forward – into his stride now
– clearing the fences like he had wings – coming up to the
seventeenth pas seul and king's nephew are out of it now –
only ever really there to make the numbers up – at the
seventeenth mill house and arkle glide over the fence – mill
house is four lengths clear – arkle's beginning to close –
this is it – time to make your move – here we go boy –
arkle's closing all the time – they're rounding the home turn
– willie robinson on mill house has the whip out – we're

there – stride for stride – the whole of cheltenham's busting
open with noise – arkle for ireland – mill house for england
– racing up to the last fence – both of them still going great
guns – arkle on the stand side mill house on the far side –
arkle jumps a length ahead – we just got to keep going now
– just keep going – but mill house makes one last attempt –
struggling to get up alongside arkle – arkle pulls away – the
war's over – arkle wins by five lengths – the greatest gold
cup ever run – i was there to see it – the day we met – up at
the airport waiting on the plane – what did i tell you

MONA. arkle was the horse to watch

DONAL. when you know something you know it

MONA. it's a pity you didn't know it about the rest of them

DONAL. we're doing alright – another thing too if that race
had've taken place in ireland it wouldn't have been the same
– it had to be here – it's better

MONA. what does it matter where it's run as long as your
horse wins

DONAL. it is better – it's like us

MONA. so you and i are like a horse race now – when i think
of us a horse race doesn't spring to mind – but there you go
– do you want another drink

DONAL. are you going to stay up when they all arrive

MONA. isn't that what you want me to do

DONAL. what do you want to do

MONA. i'm staying up

DONAL. good girl – i'll have another drink with you then

MONA. as if you wouldn't have had anyway

DONAL. i would've waited until they arrived – i don't like
sitting drinking too much on my own – you know that

MONA. you'd drink it out of a piss pot donal – (*She pours
them both a drink.*)

DONAL. that may be but not on my own – you're the lonely
pint – i'm mister social me

MONA. you know nothing

DONAL. aye – i know what i know

MONA. i wouldn't have had a drink tonight only for you

DONAL. alright – alright – you're right it's my fault – god forbid i should want you to join in in my happiness

MONA. don't start donal – i'm having the drink aren't i – what's the point in asking me and then spoiling it by chipping in my ear about it

DONAL. you're right – sorry – look – whenever the baby wakes later on looking for a feed i'll look after him – i'll sort that out – you don't have to worry about that now – i'll take care of it

MONA. donal you wouldn't know which end to stick the bottle in

DONAL. at the time just show me what to do and i'll do it

MONA. don't talk stupid

DONAL. i will

MONA. right

DONAL. right – i can look after my own child you know

MONA. that's what you do then

DONAL. and sure if he's still awake after a while bring him into the party – let them all see what a beautiful son we have – tell him in years to come – when you were a baby son we had you at parties and everyone thought you were a wee dote – he can listen to you singing – he loves that

MONA. i'm not singing tonight

DONAL. you will – they all love it

MONA. we'll see

DONAL. and it wasn't that we were like a horse race by the way

MONA. what are you talking about now

DONAL. arkle winning on english soil is like us being here

MONA. in what way would that be donal – every time you've
a drink in you it's always the same – you talk the biggest
load of cobblers

DONAL. right – say we had have met in belfast instead of here

MONA. we did meet in belfast

DONAL. very good – you know what i mean – if we had have
met in belfast our lives would have been different

MONA. it would be a strange thing if they weren't

DONAL. i know i know – right – we'd have been married

MONA. that wouldn't be a certainty

DONAL. how would it not be a certainty

MONA. being on our own in london brought us together –
quicker – in belfast that wouldn't have happened – we
wouldn't have been on our own – that might have made a
difference

DONAL. that's just for the sake of argument is it

MONA. just for the sake of argument donal

DONAL. sake of argument or not don't know if i like that
thought – for the sake of argument then say we were
married – we had kieran – you were at home and i was
doing what i'm doing – a good life – you agree

MONA. yes – and what

DONAL. the same life is better here than it is there – i'm not
talking about better or worse places i don't mean that

MONA. although belfast is worse

DONAL. you say that – i don't know – what i mean is it's
better to succeed away from home than it is at home

MONA. is that all you were saying

DONAL. it is – but i was trying to link it in with the arkle
thing and you weren't allowing me to do that – so we
wouldn't have been married then in belfast

MONA. i have you worried now don't i

DONAL. it was you that kissed me first

MONA. you filled me full of drink

DONAL. you kissed me because you were drunk is that what you're saying

MONA. yes

DONAL. yes – i filled you full of nothing by the way

MONA. you and the drink donal – it was all too much for me it just went to my head – (*She kisses him.*)

DONAL. right that's the last time – the new rule is you can't kiss me whenever you have a drink on you – (*She kisses him.*) – last last time

MONA (*her arms around him*). donal

DONAL. alright i shall make an exception this time but it's only because

MONA. because why

DONAL. you're putting pressure on me here – i can't think why

MONA. you can't keep away from me that's why

They kiss.

Scene Four

1966. DONAL *and* MONA*'s flat. The place is in a mess from a party the night before.* MONA *is asleep at the table.* DONAL *enters from work. He looks haggard. He scans the debris, pours himself a drink and knocks it back in one. He wakes* MONA.

MONA. when did you get back

DONAL. i'm just in this minute

MONA. is it tea time – didn't think i was sleeping that long

DONAL. it's as well it's not seeing you've made nothing – i left early – where's kieran

MONA. over the way playing with his wee friend

DONAL. has he been over there all day

MONA. i didn't send him over – she come over and asked if kieran could play with her son

DONAL. could you not have tidied up a bit

MONA. donal shut up

DONAL. this is what it's like then during the day is it – i go out to work and you sit here and cure your hangover with a few drinks and a kip

MONA. piss off – pour me a drink my head's splitting open

He pours the two of them a drink.

DONAL. my own head's busting – good party though – have to stop people giving kieran money when he sings – three years of age the wee lad earns a small fortune – people will think we're beggars

MONA. it's you that pushes him up to sing

DONAL. he's a good voice

MONA. he just likes being there – listening to the laughter and talking and that – you shouldn't push him forward

DONAL. he loves it – be good for him to look back on when he's older – don't like children that are wall flowers

MONA. he's only a child – starting nursery soon anyway – he can't be up to all hours then

DONAL. i know that – dave and doris are a bit

MONA. what

DONAL. don't know – don't get me wrong i like them – it's just he's a typical insurance man isn't he – cautious or something

MONA. i think he knows that now donal – you told him often enough – you also explained to him how all insurance was a con

DONAL. it is – the man needed to be told that

MONA. i like him – he's funny

DONAL. i noticed that

MONA. what does that mean

DONAL. nothing – you just talked to him a lot

MONA. they're guests in our home what am i supposed to do

DONAL. you talked to him more than you talked to her

MONA. i like him more than i like her – anyway you were talking to her

DONAL. you get too friendly when you've a drink in you

MONA. jesus christ – you're right i do and because of that after the dogs tonight don't be bringing anyone back here – i'm not up to it – we'll just tidy this place up – have a quiet night – we'll just sit and have a few drinks and relax

DONAL. i'm not going to the dogs tonight

MONA. what's wrong george not laying a book

DONAL. he is

MONA. that's good – you should take a night off now and again – between working in the office – race meetings – and the dogs – it's as if we only ever meet at parties

DONAL. i didn't take the night off mona

MONA. i don't understand – you said he was laying a book

DONAL. he told me i should take a break from clerking for him

MONA. isn't that good

DONAL. how the hell is it good – half of what i earn i earn from clerking – he told me this afternoon to go home early – he said that i was of no use to him today and that i was to go home

MONA. he knows you're hung over from last night that's all

DONAL. i told him i was fine – he just said go home – then he came off with this crack about not clerking for him

MONA. why

DONAL. try and clear your head for a minute – why do you bloody think – i'm half drunk most of the time

MONA. not during the day when you're in the office

DONAL. i get up in the morning hung over – we get up in the morning hung over

MONA. don't put this on me this is about you – and not every day

DONAL. no mona it used to be not every day – now it's every day

MONA. you not me

DONAL. jesus – shut up and listen

MONA. don't tell me to shut up

DONAL. just listen – i go into work hung over – i open the office up – mark the boards up – get the papers sorted out – everything's ready for the day's racing – i have a few drinks at lunch time – during the afternoon's work i might nip into the club for one – racing over – close the place up – call in for a drink before i come home – get my dinner – have a drink with you – get ready for the dogs – have a few drinks on the way there – clerk – have a few drinks on the way back – i arrive here with a few punters – we have a party and drink to all hours – you starting to get the picture – am i painting this clearly enough for you

MONA. and what about george – you're with him most of the time – he does the exact same thing – there's no way he can say that he doesn't

DONAL. he doesn't have to say a damn thing he owns the place – i only manage it – he's the boss man

MONA. why all this now – what's changed all of a sudden – you didn't say anything to him did you – telling him how to run his business – and how much of a big man you are

DONAL. he's made good money out of me – he's the one with the cash – i'm the one with the knowledge – he knows that

MONA. maybe he just doesn't like you spitting it in his face all the time

DONAL. maybe he doesn't

MONA. did he say that

DONAL. yes

MONA. stop bloody doing it then – it's not difficult to figure out is it

DONAL. it's not that easy

MONA. not that easy how – is he going to sack you

DONAL. no – he wouldn't sack me – i said to him am i not doing my job – he said you're the best i know at your job

MONA. always the best – what's his problem then

DONAL. he said because of my drinking that my behaviour while i was clerking was having an adverse effect on the punters – they see me drunk on the box and think i'm incapable – so they punt elsewhere – simple as that

MONA. he'll be alright donal – have a word with him – he knows what the situation is in your game – hand in hand – (*Pours herself a drink.*) it's not right to punish someone for having a drink is it

DONAL (*knocks the drink out of her hand*). you're not listening to me

MONA. what the hell did you do that for

DONAL. you're not listening to me

MONA. i was listening – there was no need for that

DONAL. understanding what i'm saying is what i mean

MONA. just take a drink and relax

DONAL. we need to talk

MONA. right – jesus donal

DONAL. i'm sorry – let's not have a drink – let the one that we've had be enough

MONA (*picking the glass up off the floor*). i want another one

DONAL. i want to talk

MONA (*pouring*). i'll talk while i'm having a drink – and i want you to have one – it's been a bad day for you – i want you to have a drink – you need one – if you don't have one i'll bear the brunt of it

DONAL. no you won't it's not like that

MONA. donal don't come that nonsense with me – take the drink (*Pours him a drink.*)

DONAL. say george is right

MONA. he's not right – he's jealous that's all – he sees you doing what you do and knows he can't do it himself – i've been in that betting office while you're working – all the punters love you – half of them wouldn't be there if you weren't there – he's an old jealous man – he comes to this flat and sees how well we get on with people – he sees that we love each other and that we're going up in the world – and he hates it – he'd sack you if he could but he knows it would be the end of his business – all that other stuff about clerking on course is nonsense – he's just nasty – a nasty wee old man – you'd be better off without him – you could walk into another job anywhere and he knows that

DONAL. it used to be that i would believe that – i don't know

MONA. well do know because it's true

DONAL. it doesn't matter whether it's true or not

MONA. how does it not – him being like that means he makes decisions about you – decisions that aren't right – decisions that you can't do anything about

DONAL. it doesn't matter because it's not about him – it's about me – it's about you and me

MONA. it is about him – you know it's about him and you won't confront him – you give off to him about all the small things but when it gets to the crunch – you don't want to know

DONAL. i don't want to know – is that right – i'll tell you about not wanting to know will i

MONA. tell me whatever you like – what difference will it make – it's him you should be telling

DONAL. after he talked to me i left the office – i'm thinking i have to have a drink and think about this – before i went into the bar i looked in through the window – wanted to make sure there was no punters there – needed to be on my own – think – didn't know anybody – good – then i caught my own reflection in the window – the place was full of drunks all there to drink the day away – all old before their time – men that once had life in them now looked small – as if the drink had shrunk them – and there was me looking at myself in the window – i hadn't noticed before but i was one of them – i look and feel ten years older than i am

MONA. you're hung over donal – don't make a drama out of something that isn't

DONAL. when i came over here and we first started going out – remember we used to walk about london all the time – always walking through crowds – it was always in my mind that you and i stuck out from the crowd – had a bit of money – the two of us dressed like we owned the place – always the best of gear – we were both healthy – fit – bright as two shiny buttons – people used to look at us – we were like movie stars – i used to imagine we didn't walk we glided – now all we do is stumble – it wasn't meant to be like this

MONA. we have a laugh – that's what we have – a laugh

DONAL. we're alcoholics

MONA. don't use that word – don't ever use that word

DONAL. not hearing it doesn't mean it's not true

MONA. it's not true – that word doesn't describe us – that's not who we are – that word belongs to other people – people who are in the gutter – people with no dignity

DONAL. it describes what we do – we drink

MONA. so now and again we go overboard – that doesn't make us bad people

DONAL. i didn't say we were bad people

MONA. yes you did – i'm not an alcoholic – and neither are you

DONAL. mona all we do is drink

MONA. you work – i look after this place and kieran

DONAL. have a look around you – the place is a kip – kieran's not here – it's the middle of the afternoon and we're having a drink

MONA. i look after kieran – don't say i don't

DONAL. how long is it going to be before he starts coming second – when he woke up this morning i was asleep on the sofa for christ sake

MONA. that was you not me

DONAL. it's not a competition mona – you have to step outside yourself sometimes and have a look – see the picture – have a look at us mona

MONA. i see who we are alright – and it's not what you're saying – say we do drink a bit too much and

DONAL. alcoholics

MONA. shut up – i mean it donal shut up

DONAL. alcoholics

MONA (*she slaps his face*). i am a person with dignity and self-respect – if what you just said is how you see me then leave now – walk out that door and don't come back – there's a difference between drinking too much and that

DONAL. no – we have to stop – it's become like breathing to us – can't you see that

MONA. i like having a drink – that's what i see – i like having a drink

DONAL. so do i – that's the point mona

MONA. and what would we do – tell me that – what would we
do

DONAL. we'd not drink – it can't be the only thing that we
have – if it is you're right one of us should walk out that
door – it can't be all we have

MONA. what would i do – what is it i have – i'm stuck in this
place on my own day after day – do you know what that's
like – no you don't – i sit and wait on you coming back
from wherever you've been with your boozing buddies – so
i can have a drink and a laugh because it's the only adult
company i've had that day – don't speak to me about what
we have

DONAL. you won't be on your own i'll be here – i'm not
clerking any more – i'll be here – me you and kieran – we'll
be here together – we live in london and we never do things
– what's the point in kieran being brought up here if he
doesn't experience that type of life – we could do that

MONA. i don't know

DONAL. we could do that – me you and kieran – no singing at
parties for him – you're right he's only a child

MONA. for him

DONAL. yes

MONA. and what about work

DONAL. i don't know – if we can get through this

MONA. why don't you leave – start up with someone else – a
fresh – maybe even do something else

DONAL. i could do that but – it's a good job – i'll leave the
situation with george for a while – then let him know i've
straightened myself out – then i'll get back to the clerking –
i'll have to we'll need the money – i know what you're
thinking – if i go back to the clerking it will all start up
again – the drinking and you being on your own – it won't
it'll be different – it'll be clerking without drinking – and
you can come to race meetings with me – that'll be the way
we wanted it to be – so we've decided – that's it no more
drink

MONA. we'll finish this bottle and then that's it

DONAL. just stop now

MONA. no – finish the bottle

DONAL. i'm not taking another one

MONA. donal you do what you want but i'm finishing what's in front of me and then that's it

DONAL. i'd prefer if

MONA. don't

DONAL. right – i'm going to go over the way and get kieran – feel like a walk – maybe bring him to the park or something – you be alright

MONA. yes

DONAL exits. MONA pours herself a drink and knocks it back.

Scene Five

1966. DONAL and MONA have just come back from the races. They are dancing round the flat.

DONAL. such a day – this is the day to be irish – we should all eat shamrock for dinner – saint patrick's day and himself wins a third gold cup – a day to be in love – (*He kisses her.*)

MONA. i have to sit down – dancing down the street all those people thought we were mad

DONAL. you could dance round the world on a day like this – if this is what mad is dear open up the doors of the nut house because i'm waltzing in

MONA. do you think kieran will be alright over there – i don't like leaving him like that

DONAL. he'll be fine – it was him that wanted to sleep over – he'll be fine – wee lad will have a ball – we have the place to ourselves – (*He kisses her again.*) – heaven i'm in heaven –

i know i keep saying it but it's true – i love this place –
what's the best thing about london

MONA. tell me

DONAL. come on the best thing

MONA. going into town and just walking about – not going
into shops or anything – just walking amongst all those
people – they don't know me and i don't know them – yet
we're all here – i like that

DONAL. yes that's a good one but that's not it – the one thing
– what is it

MONA. big buildings

DONAL. yes but no

MONA. the river

DONAL. i love the river

MONA. it would nearly make you want to jump into it

DONAL. i don't love it that much

MONA. straight off westminster bridge in your swimsuit –
straight in like an arrow

DONAL. the best thing about london is – the tube

MONA. no – the best thing is walking above the ground not
going under the ground

DONAL. what have we been here – four years – and you still
know nothing – the underground – the tube – the best thing
a person that god pumped breath into ever invented –
london has the best transport system in the world – not that
i've been round the world but i bet you it has – to go down
under the ground get on a train then a few minutes later
come up and you're halfway across town – if they had a
tube line to cheltenham that would be perfect – cheltenham
– thirty lengths – how does a horse win by thirty lengths

MONA. don't get me wrong about this donal – i know how
much you love arkle – and the racing was very good – i
really enjoyed it – that main race – the gold cup – did it not

seem a bit pointless – everybody knew that horse was going to win and it won – where's the excitement in that

DONAL. if the possibility of defeat doesn't exist what drives your interest is the magnitude of victory – a wiser man than me once said that – what i will say is – you have to feel sorry for the other horses really – they must look at arkle in the paddock and think – oh god no – bet you the other horses call himself himself – there's nothing ever pointless about being in the presence of the best

MONA. i'll tell you one thing – i didn't know they ran that fast

DONAL. speeding bullets – did you see him going through that fence – i've never seen anything like that before in my life – any other horse be dead – arkle's blessed though – he's immortal – he just ran through it like it wasn't there

MONA. he was looking at the crowd – i saw him – forgot the fence was there he did

DONAL. straight through it – you know why all those people are there – it's not to have a punt – i mean the horse was ten to one on – no amount of readies does you any good at that price – history in the making – they witnessed history in the making – we witnessed history in the making – should've brought the wee lad too young or not – although arkle will be about for years – he'll get seeing him some time – get him to do a few bets for me he'd like that

MONA. that child's never going to do what you do donal – i wouldn't let it happen

DONAL. i was just talking about bringing him to the races – that's all

MONA. i just wanted to make that clear that's all

DONAL. what's wrong with what i do

MONA. for you nothing – for him everything – it's not the world i want him to live in – i mean it – this is our world – our world can't be his world

DONAL. i was talking to george earlier on

MONA. what was he saying – give you a pat on the back did he for being a good boy – i see you have remained on the straight and narrow donal – well done – i truly respect you as a person now – yeah

DONAL. don't be like that – i'm back clerking with him – he didn't have to do that

MONA. yes he did – what was he saying

DONAL. it's good – it's very good – something that we need to talk about – something that has to be talked about in a serious way – we have to

MONA. talk about it then instead of bubbling on

DONAL. i don't bubble on

MONA. you always bubble on – just say the thing

DONAL. he wants me to become his partner

MONA. serious

DONAL. see – i said it was serious – talked about in a serious way

MONA. what exactly did he say – you didn't get it wrong did you

DONAL. don't be bloody stupid how could i get it wrong – it wasn't like it was a drunken conversation was it – he said that he admired the fact that i had got my act together – it showed that i was thinking about my future seriously – that i was somebody that could be trusted because i had put working within his business before myself – that was a big thing for him to say – then he said because he was getting older he wanted to work less and have a bit less responsibility – that meant having a partner – and because he didn't have a son of his own to pass the thing on to – he wondered whether i'd be interested

MONA. what you say

DONAL. i said i'd have to talk to you

MONA. did you really say that or have you already said to him – if you have don't lie

DONAL. i don't lie – i didn't say to him – he didn't want me to answer there and then anyway – what do you think

MONA. what would it all mean

DONAL. commitment – we'd have to make up our minds this is where we're staying

MONA. have we not already done that – we're here aren't we

DONAL. permanent

MONA. yes permanent

DONAL. we'd have to get a bank loan – i don't know how difficult that would be – it's a good business and i'm sure as long as the bank know that it'll be alright – george would help me out there anyway i think

MONA. i think you should go for it – what was it you used to say to me – there's a reason why bookies live in big houses

DONAL. i'd be a bookie – just think about that – i'd be a bookie

MONA. you are a bookie

DONAL. no – i work for a bookie – this time i'd be a bookie

MONA. isn't that what you want

DONAL. is it what you want

MONA. we can only sort out what each of us wants one at a time

DONAL. you sure about that

MONA. yes

DONAL. thank you – decided

MONA. decided

DONAL. big decisions – this is a moment isn't it

MONA. it is – maybe the biggest one yet

DONAL. right – right – what i'm going to suggest now may seem like the wrong thing to do – but it isn't – i just have to get something – hold on – (*He exits then returns with a bottle of whisky and sets it on the table.*)

MONA. donal

DONAL. listen listen listen

MONA. where'd you get that from

DONAL. i had it hidden in the bedroom

MONA. since when

DONAL. does that matter

MONA. yes

DONAL. it's not open

MONA. i can see that

DONAL. the day after we decided to go off the drink – a back-up – in case i needed it – but i never did

MONA. why didn't you tell me

DONAL. because it had to do with me not you – plus i didn't want you blowing your top

MONA. i don't blow my top

DONAL. yes you do

MONA. i thought we were doing this together

DONAL. we were – we are – just listen a minute

MONA. hold on a second – (*She goes to a cupboard gets a bottle of whisky from it and sets it on the table.*)

DONAL. i thought we were doing this together

MONA. we were – we are

Laughter.

DONAL. we've earned this

MONA (*unscrewing the top*). yes

DONAL. wait wait

MONA. what

DONAL. we have to know why we're doing this

MONA. you just said – we've earned it

DONAL. this isn't going back – we're not going back

MONA. shut up – don't spoil things donal

DONAL. i'm not – we're going to have a laugh

MONA. there'd be no point otherwise

DONAL. it's just – i have to say

MONA. alright – alright – say what you have to say and that's it – you see – bubbling again

DONAL. when george was talking to me today – after he said what he had to say – he asked me did i want to have a beer – that was two things – it was a test right – but also he was seeing could i be trusted just to take the one and not end up going out on a bender – i didn't take the drink – i wanted to but i didn't – the reason was i wanted to have a drink with you – it was a good day and i wanted us to celebrate it – we can do this – we can have a drink like normal punters – civilised

MONA. is that it – are you finished

DONAL. yes – but that's it isn't it – i'm right aren't i

MONA. yes

DONAL. tell me why you're doing this – i need to know

MONA. because i'm bored – at this moment in time does it really matter why donal – all we need to know is that we can handle it – and we've shown each other that we can – neither of the bottles were open

DONAL. that's right neither of the bottles were open

MONA *pours them both a drink.*

MONA. to good health and happiness

DONAL. good health and happiness

They knock them back and pour another two. DONAL *starts to dance, the same way as they did years ago on Westminster Bridge.* MONA *applauds.*

DONAL. where do bookies live

MONA. in big houses

DONAL. better believe it darling

MONA *dances on the chair and drinks from the bottle.*

Scene Six

The following morning. DONAL *and* MONA *are both in a drunken sleep.* DONAL *wakes. He puts the bottle beside him to his head but there is nothing in it. He searches the room for more drink but there is none. There is a knock at the door. He ignores it. He wakes* MONA.

DONAL. get up you

MONA. what time is it

DONAL. don't know

MONA. was there somebody knocking the door there

DONAL. yes – it was your woman with kieran – don't want any of that yet

MONA. no – anything left in that bottle

DONAL. no – you must've drank the last drop in it

MONA. piss off

DONAL. well it wasn't me – always leave a drop in it for the morning – that's what i do you know that

MONA. that's what you think you do – that's what you say you do – you never do it

DONAL. i do do it – you've no discipline – that's what's wrong with you – that's why you're a bad person to have a drink with

MONA. go out and get some

DONAL. it's sunday everything's shut – what type of nonsense is that shutting everything – has it to do with god

MONA. stop talking my head's busting

DONAL. jesus took a drink didn't he – the last supper were they not all banging wine into them – alright for jesus not alright for us – go to mass get a wee bit of wine with communion – just enough to wet your whistle – get the taste of it on your tongue – will we go to mass and dip our tongues in the wine

MONA. you're useless – that's what's wrong – it's you – you have no plans in your head – plus you talk a lot of nonsense

DONAL. i have plans

MONA. no you don't – you don't look after me – you think you do but you don't

DONAL. stop talking like that – it's not funny – it's not clever – why do you have to be like that – i was joking there – then you have to sort of change everything – you have to make it like it's important or something

MONA. see that's what i mean

DONAL. what

MONA. it is important – our life is important – and you're useless

DONAL. the drink's still in your head – you see this is what i mean about discipline – be careful what you say – don't just let it spill out – this can go the wrong way you know that

MONA. don't threaten me

DONAL. don't do this then

MONA. i need a drink

DONAL. you shouldn't have drank the last drop – stick to the plan – no discipline – have you any more bottles hidden

MONA. i have no discipline – therefore i am not able to hide anything – not only are you useless you're stupid – why if i need a drink would i know that there is a bottle hidden somewhere and not go and get it

DONAL. i'll tell you why – because if you got it you'd have to share it with me – you'd rather have none than share it – that's the way your mind's gone

MONA. that would be the type of thing you'd do

DONAL. if you have a bottle get it out

MONA. if you have a bottle you get it out

DONAL. i don't have one

MONA. neither do i

DONAL. i don't believe you

MONA. i don't believe you

DONAL. you're the liar i'm not the liar

MONA. where do you get that from – liar

DONAL. you lied to me that you didn't have a wee thing in your head for dave

MONA. jesus christ donal don't start this again

DONAL. you did

MONA. he was a nice man – i liked talking to him – i liked talking to her as well – you spent plenty of time talking to her didn't you

DONAL. that's different – i meant nothing by it – you frightened him off – that's why they stopped coming round here

MONA. they stopped coming round here because you tortured them – you get drunk and then you just won't let go – right up into people's faces – hounding them – getting them to talk about things they don't want to talk about – you put people under pressure donal they don't like that

DONAL. people don't like you

MONA. is that it – is that the best you can do

DONAL. they don't

MONA. dave did apparently

DONAL. no he didn't – frightened him – all over him like a rash – drink changes you for the worse

MONA. changes me does it – what friends have you got other than the people you work with – none – why – because you're a pain in the arse

DONAL. you're doing it again – this is it now – right – go and get the bottle

MONA. there is no bottle donal

DONAL. i tried but you kept pushing it – you crossed the line – go get the bottle

MONA. go out and hunt – that's what you're meant to be isn't it – a hunter-gatherer thing – i'm here looking after the young – it's your job to feed us – you'd make a bloody useless caveman you know that

DONAL. sometimes i look at you and what i see is a stink – there's a smell of bile from you – i can see it like a gas floating around you – clinging to your skin – see if you don't tell me where that bottle is i'm going to wreck this place – and you along with it – i know you – you hid one bottle which means you had two

MONA. wreck the place – wreck away – donal things aren't a threat if you've seen it all before – it loses its power – there is no element of surprise

DONAL. where's the bottle

MONA. there is no bottle

DONAL *throws a chair across the room and turns the table upside down.* MONA *throws her chair across the room*

DONAL. you'd rather do this than get the bottle

MONA. if you're going to hit me – hit me – don't lay the blame for that on me

DONAL *punches her, knocking her to the floor. He kicks her while she is lying there. He moves away from her. He gets a chair and sits on it.* MONA *picks herself up. She takes money from her handbag. Walks to* DONAL *and puts the money in his hand.*

MONA. what a man – go you out now with money and get drunk – go and tell people how you keep your woman under control

DONAL. there's rules – even for the likes of us there's rules – you didn't stick by the rules – that all suited you – don't think i don't know that – it's not just me

MONA. hunter gatherer

> DONAL *exits.* MONA *gets a bottle of drink from behind the cupboard.*

Scene Seven

1968. DONAL *is addressing an A.A. meeting for the first time. During this speech we see* MONA *alone on Westminster Bridge. She is drinking from a hip flask while looking down into the water.*

DONAL. my name is donal mackin and – and i am an
   alcoholic – the problem with talking like this – i know that
   you have all done this – and that i won't be judged – i had a
   feeling that would make this easier – but it isn't – maybe
   that's it – maybe you need to do it and then it will be easier
   – it's just – i don't want to say things i don't want to say –
   yet i know deep down those are the things i need to say –
   need to get out into the open – there are other people
   involved – and i don't know how fair it is to mention them
   when they are not here – i have a wife and a son – i feel like
   i have taken them on this journey – i feel like i am a good
   man – yet i don't act like a good man – i don't put enough
   effort into the right type of living to make me a good man –
   that's what good people do – they put effort into a normal
   type of living – i think that's what they do – i don't know –
   maybe i don't even know any good people – i thought so
   much about myself i haven't noticed who's been around me
   – i'm sorry i know i don't seem to be making any sense – i
   – my wife is an alcoholic as well – she doesn't see it like
   that – but she is – she thinks all this is just a matter of self-
   discipline and dignity – she didn't want me to come here –
   i can understand why i didn't want to come myself – she
   shouted at me before i left the house this evening – i feel
   like i've let her down in some way – not in some way –
   i have let her down – i have let both of them down in
   different ways – her because i'm doing this on my own –
   and him because i haven't taken proper notice of him – like

all children he's been telling me about his world – and i
haven't been listening to him – that's the thing i feel saddest
about – it's also the thing that frightens me most – that i
have put him second – put everything way down the list –
except for drink of course – i don't really want to talk about
my wife and child – i've said enough about that – this has to
be about me – i know that – that's why i'm here – although
in saying that i don't really know how i got here – i do – it's
because i had nowhere else to go – i mean i don't know
how i got to this point – it feels like it has all just passed me
by or something – one minute i've arrived in london to start
a new life and the next it's over six years on and i'm
explaining myself at an a a meeting – everything was good
– it couldn't have been better – married to the woman i love
– a beautiful child – and a good job – a job that i liked
doing – i had a future – it was as if the drinking caught up
with me – i was drinking to be sociable – that's what i
thought – it was always part and parcel of what i did – i am
– was – a bookie – we were having a ball – people – drink –
activity – there was always activity – i always thought that
was a good thing – doesn't seem like that now – i
sometimes ask myself was it because i was in london –
because i was away from home – i'm from belfast – would
it have been the same if i had've stayed in belfast – that's
not something you can answer is it – something changed in
me – i can see that now – i don't really know how to
explain this – but it's like life being good isn't really
enough – it's as if you go out of your way to make things
more difficult for yourself – what you think you're doing is
making the world a better place – what you're really doing
is the opposite of that – the strange thing is i knew i was
doing it – i knew i was making things worse – you can't
help yourself – it's not just drink – it's about understanding
yourself or something – i don't know – i haven't worked
that out yet – maybe that's something you never work out –
maybe the journey or the struggle or whatever it is is a
lifelong thing – i don't know what's going to happen to me
– i just know something has to happen

MONA *finishes what is left in the hip flask then lets it drop
into the river.*

Scene Eight

*1969. A grubby hotel room. There are bottles of drink
everywhere, some empty, some not. MONA is curled up on the
bed, drunk. DONAL enters. He surveys the room then sits on a
chair and looks at MONA.*

DONAL (*standing over her*). mona

MONA. go away from me

DONAL. mona wake up

MONA. oh – it's you – go home donal

DONAL. no

MONA. how did you find me

DONAL. i got a phone call from one of your drinking partners
– said you were in a state – he was worried

MONA. was he – there are some decent men left in the world
– decent men donal – not that decent in that he didn't stay
though – can't trust men donal – men are not to be trusted –
(*Drinks from a bottle.*) – go home donal – just go home

DONAL. i want you to come home with me

MONA. home – i'm not going anywhere – this is home – i
have a ball here – this is where i want to be – need to be
here donal

DONAL. kieran wants you to come home

MONA. where is he – no doubt staying across the way with
his auntie may and his wee friend – she thinks she owns
him now does she – well she doesn't own him he's mine

DONAL. ours

MONA. ours – why didn't you bring him with you

DONAL. do you really want him to see you like this

MONA. yes – yes – i do – i want him to see me like this – i
want him to see the way you look at me – i want him to see
the love in our eyes donal – ha ha – that's what i want him
to see – miss me did you

DONAL. yes

MONA. no you didn't – don't lie to me

DONAL. why am i here then

MONA. oh i don't know – maybe you have the need to save another soul – not content with saving your own you have to interfere with others – isn't that the way it works – go tell those people you talk to that i'm a lost cause – go tell them this soul's not for saving

DONAL. i don't tell anyone anything mona

MONA. i don't tell anyone anything mona – god you're pathetic – you make me sick you know that – i used to look at you and see a man – now all i see is you – a child – a child that won't do what he wants for fear of offending his wee group

DONAL. i am doing what i want – i'm just not doing what you want

MONA. well you should do what i want – it's me mona – mona – the one that's been with you all along – do what i want – have a drink with me

DONAL. no

MONA. i'll let you take me if you have a drink with me – is that a fair deal – fair exchange is no robbery

DONAL. that the normal price now is it

MONA. piss off – you know nothing – what would it matter to you if it was anyway – you wouldn't be man enough to take it up

DONAL. i don't like you talking like this

MONA (*stands up, takes a drink and moves close to him*). come to bed with me – show me you love me

DONAL. this is all it is is it – this is how it ends up

MONA. yes this is how it ends up – me and you – a bottle – and a few laughs

DONAL. there's no laughs here – maybe you can hear them i can't

MONA. i need a man donal – are you a man – can't you see me – a woman – a woman calling out to you

DONAL. i see a drunk on a bender – confused – come home with me

MONA. go to hell – you're useless – useless to me – on your way out send someone in – someone who's of use to me

DONAL. stop talking like that

MONA. you not like that – forgive me i'm confused – don't want me yourself but don't like the idea of anyone else wanting me

DONAL. i do want you

MONA. then show me

DONAL. not like this – not now

MONA. don't want to take advantage of me – take advantage of me – show me you're a person – a real person instead of just a bunch of good thoughts – (*Up close to his face.*) come on take advantage of me

DONAL. stop it

MONA. i know you can do it – i know who you are – i've seen you suck the carpet because you needed the taste of drink in your mouth

DONAL. shut up

MONA. oh yes – i've seen you piss over the child's bed because you didn't know what room you were in

DONAL. i'm warning you

MONA. you're a bad person donal – take advantage of me – we both know it isn't the first time

He strikes her across the face and she falls to the floor.

DONAL. bitch

MONA. you like that (*She stands up.*) that's it is it

She hits him in the face. He strikes her again then trails her by the hair and throws her on the bed. He pulls her skirt up

then gets on top of her. He pushes himself against her. He grabs her by the hair and pulls her face up to his. For a moment they freeze. He lets go of her hair and rolls off the bed onto the floor.

DONAL. i don't know what it is you want me to do – i've tried everything – there isn't anything else i know to do

MONA. no not everything

DONAL. why are you asking me to do the one thing i can't

MONA. because it's the one thing i need – you've abandoned me

DONAL. i'm here

MONA. you've abandoned me – you brought me into this world – you owe me

DONAL. you walked in with your eyes open

She sits beside him and puts his head in her lap.

MONA. it'll be alright

DONAL. will it – we're just two paddies in london aren't we – that's what this story is

MONA. no – we're two people together – who look after each other

DONAL. yeah – looking after each other

MONA. we can do that – we've always done that

She takes a drink then hands him the bottle.

DONAL. to your health and happiness – (*He takes a long drink from the bottle.*) – maybe we should go back to belfast

MONA. why

DONAL. i don't know

MONA. no – our home's here now

DONAL. maybe so – (*He takes another long drink then hands the bottle to* MONA.) did you ever think what it would be like being a horse

MONA. no – never thought what it would be like to be any
  animal – when i was a child i always thought what it would
  be like to be someone else – i always talked about what age
  people were – i was always asking people their age – then i
  would ask them what it was like being them – and did they
  like being them – then i would ask them if they would like
  to be me – and sometimes they would say i don't know
  what's it like being you – i would always say the same thing
  – it's alright – i never once said it was good – always just
  it's alright – i was only six or seven at the time – it used to
  amuse people – except my father – he used to tell me that
  i was only a child and that i should stop talking like a
  grown-up – i always found that strange – because i never
  heard a grown-up talk like that – even though i was very
  young that made me think that adults must think like that
  even though they don't say it – how else would my father
  know that i was talking like an adult – (*Takes a drink.*) – i
  was a funny child – why a horse – because of the racing

DONAL. not any horse

MONA. arkle

DONAL. arkle – what is it like to be arkle – does he know he's
  arkle – does he know how brave he is – coming up to a
  fence – with the rain beating against his face – and the mud
  flying about the place – does he know that he could hit the
  fence – fall arse over hoof and his neck snap like a twig –
  coming up to a fence does he say to himself – i must be
  brave – is that what happens – does he say to himself i'm a
  hero – i'm a hero and i have to be brave even though i'm
  frightened – or is it just a horse jumping fences because he
  doesn't know any different – a dumb animal doing
  something for no other reason than it's there to do – isn't
  something you could ever know is it – what's it like to be
  arkle

MONA. if you can't ever know it – you have to make a choice
  about what you believe

DONAL. i believe he's brave – i need to do that

Scene Nine

1970. DONAL *is in the flat, wrapping objects in newspaper and putting them in boxes.* MONA *enters. She is wearing a shabby overcoat. She looks haggard and drawn.*

MONA. hi

DONAL. right – it's been a while mona – longest yet

MONA. it was best i stayed away – i thought – i knew it was the best thing

DONAL. that was decent of you

MONA. i don't want – don't want to – why are you packing

DONAL. why do you think – we're moving

MONA. weren't you going to tell me – just go like that – i need to know that you're here

DONAL. we stay trapped in this one spot because you need to know we're here – that's not the way it works any more

MONA. you were just going to run off without telling me

DONAL. no – i tried to find you mona but you weren't in the usual places

MONA. no – how is kieran

DONAL. kieran's fine – he asks where you are now and again

MONA. what do you tell him

DONAL. oh don't worry i don't tell him the truth

MONA. what do you tell him

DONAL. i tell him that we both love him – but that some times grown-ups need to spend some time apart – i tell him none of this is his fault

MONA. i do love him

DONAL. he needed more than that

MONA. i haven't had a drink in three days

DONAL. right

MONA. that's what i came round to tell you – i wanted to tell you that just so you would know

DONAL. where are you staying

MONA. i have a bedsit on the other side of town – not a great deal to look at – just one room – i've been sitting by myself in it for the last three days – i just thought i'd come round and say that

DONAL. i didn't throw you out mona – you left – the fact that you sit in a room on your own for three days isn't me punishing you – you left

MONA. i know that – i know that – i just wanted you to know that i'm trying – you don't have to say anything about that – i just wanted you to know that's all

DONAL. there isn't much for me to say – i've said it all

MONA. donal i know – i just wanted to tell you – (*Pause.*) – i walked over westminster bridge on the way here – i had forgotten how beautiful london looks at night – the lights shining on the river – the size of the buildings – i think that's what attracts people here in the first place – the size of the place – all these people coming from smaller places to be part of the big place – remember the day we first arrived here – walking around for hours – amazed how big everything was – i forgot that – it's easy to forget things isn't it

DONAL. sometimes it is mona yes

MONA. donal i'm sorry that i forgot things

DONAL. mona you don't have to

MONA. i want to say this – i'm sorry that i forgot how things could be between us – there was a time when everything was right

DONAL. was there

MONA. yes there was – the three of us here together in london on our own – happy – there were times when i should've forced myself to remember that and i didn't

DONAL. you shouldn't have to force yourself to remember good times

MONA. you know what i mean – don't start the preaching – you've been where i am – there are days when you have to force yourself to breathe – you know that – i know you have difficulty feeling sympathy for me but don't pretend you don't know what i'm talking about

DONAL. you're right – i do have difficulty feeling sympathy for you

MONA. do you hate me

DONAL. no

MONA. do you love me – you don't have to answer

DONAL. why'd you ask it then

MONA. i don't know – maybe because i've been sitting in a room on my own for three days – and before that no other human being has taken any notice of me for weeks

DONAL. yes i love you

MONA. what if

DONAL. don't

MONA. why not

DONAL. mona kieran and i are moving back to belfast – moving back for good

MONA. you were just going to leave me here

DONAL. i told you i tried to find you

MONA. you can't – i don't understand – you were going to leave me here – you were going to take my son and just leave

DONAL. our son

MONA. no you're not doing it – how can you tell me you love me and then do something like that

DONAL. how can you leave us and go on the drink for months at a time – don't come that crack with me – i'm doing what's best – i'm not doing it to hurt you

MONA. yes you are you fucker – you pretend to forgive but
you don't – you're full of spite and hate – you're not doing
it – i won't let you do it

DONAL. how are you going to stop me

MONA. he's my child

DONAL. he's our child

MONA. i'll get the authorities on to you

DONAL. we're leaving tomorrow – getting the boat – that
sums everything up about this doesn't it – arrive on a plane
leave on a boat

MONA. i'll get the police now tell them you're kidnapping my
son

DONAL. mona nobody gives a damn about us – get the
authorities involved and what

MONA. i'll tell them how you treated me – how much of a
bastard you are – a child has to be with its mother

DONAL. why weren't you here then – people ask questions –
they'll ask kieran what type of life he's lead – brought up
by two drunks that'll be the picture painted – they'll take
him away from both of us

MONA. a child needs its mother

DONAL. what's the choice here – you think it's best he stays
here with you

MONA. stay here

DONAL. i'm not staying here – i can't

MONA. then fuck off and leave me with my son

DONAL. i'm sober and you're a clapped-out drunken ole
whore

She attempts to hit him and he stops her. She spits at him.

MONA. i've been in the company of other men – but i was
never with them – you know that you hurtful bastard

DONAL. how do i know what you've done

MONA. because you know me – you're the only person knows me – this is what this is about isn't it

DONAL. no

MONA. it is – you want to hurt me by taking kieran away

DONAL. it's about doing the right thing – my time here has finished – it's over – arkle's dead

MONA. i don't understand – what do you mean – you're going back to belfast because some racehorse is dead – are you mad – has staying sober made you mad – it's only a horse

DONAL. i know that – this has to do with me – i was reading the paper last week – the headline on the back page was arkle is dead – and it just made me think – it's over here – my time here is finished – i don't belong here – i have no right being here any more – it's time to go home

MONA. tell me – when you were reading your paper did it mention anything about home – did it mention the lovely belfast

DONAL. it's home mona

MONA. they're murdering each other over there donal – there's soldiers on the streets – people are being burnt out of their homes – people have been shot dead – none of that is going to get any better – do the right thing – you want to put our son in the middle of all that – that's the right thing is it – kieran's english donal – belfast isn't his home

DONAL. it'll become his home – the situation isn't perfect i know that – but it's better than staying here

MONA. tell me how the hell it's better than staying here

DONAL. staying here only really made sense to me when we were together

MONA. that's not a good enough reason donal

DONAL. i can't do this here on my own – it's too hard

MONA. do what – live

DONAL. live staying sober

MONA. we'll do it together

DONAL. i can't do that either – i'm not strong enough mona

MONA. why can't it go back to the way it was – it was just a bit of fun

DONAL. that's what scares me – it would be too easy to fool myself into thinking we could get it back to the way it was – whenever i was out looking for you to tell you what i was going to do i was frightened – i was frightened that i was going to find you

MONA. donal don't

DONAL. no listen – i was frightened that i was going to find you with another man

MONA. donal i already told you – there is only you

DONAL. i'm just explaining to you how i felt – then i was frightened that i would find you in the gutter somewhere – and to look at you lying there would break my heart – but the thing that frightened me the most was the thing i wanted the most – that i would find you in a bar – on your own – not yet drunk – that you were in that place that was warm – soft – comfort – the place that makes us happy – and that i would sit down beside you and we would have a drink together – and we would smile – that's what frightened me the most – we don't know any different mona – it's then that we're at our best – i can't do it any more – i just can't

MONA. i don't want you to leave donal – i can't be on my own

DONAL. that's the only way we can be mona – we aren't good for each other – do you know why arkle was the greatest

MONA. shut up about the damn horse

DONAL. it was well managed – it wasn't just that it had talent – it was well looked after

MONA. i never thought we would end – i never thought that

DONAL. neither did i

MONA. i don't want us to end

DONAL. neither do i – there isn't any other way though

MONA. kieran – donal – kieran

DONAL. tell me i'm not doing the right thing

MONA. a bedsit's no place for a child is it – i – i have to go –
i – i have to go

DONAL. why don't you go in and say hello to kieran – it'll be
alright to wake him up – he'd like to see you

MONA. oh god no – i ah – i don't want him to see me like this
– i look a mess i know i do – tell him – tell him i called
round to see him but he was sleeping – tell him i gave him a
kiss goodnight while he was sleeping – tell him that

DONAL. of course i will

MONA. tell him i'll write to him and that he – he ah – he has
to write back to me

DONAL. mona

MONA. just tell him that – i have to go now – three days donal
– three days is good

DONAL. yeah – look after yourself

MONA *exits.*

DONAL *continues his packing.*